the wild in-between

NICOLE COLINAREZ

PAPER LION PRESS
WWW.PAPERLIONPRESS.COM

for eric,

most ardently.

xo, n.

Copyright © 2018 Nicole Colinarez. All rights reserved.

Printed in the United States of America.

ISBN: 978-0-9974164-9-7

CONTENTS

WAYWARD HEARTS   *4*

WOLVES   *69*

SIRENS   *109*

LIGHTHOUSES   *165*

ACKNOWLEDGEMENTS   *208*

AUTHOR   *209*

WAYWARD HEARTS

– and what we seek in the darkness –

it's all
lighthouses

and

harbors
until bowlines
break

and

drowning
isn't an option.

— life raft not included

we move mountains

with tears

and wonder why

no one

believes

in

Atlantis

anymore.

— the priestesses cried

no one headlines

the top 5 tricks

to silencing

the voice inside–

its siren song

spoken

with a forked tongue–

whispering

it is better to

starve

than be fat,

it is better to be

invisible

than flawed.

— how dare you love yourself

i just

think

it is

time

i stop

cutting

myself

open

to get to

the stories.

— i pick at my scars

your love line
is cut short,

she says,
running her finger
across my palm.

i know,

i say,

i never meant for
that wound to scar.

— hearts are bloody things

let's pretend,
for the night,

that you never hurt me

and

i never hurt you

and

love is actually enough.

— we both know it never is; some day we'll grow up

i know why

waves crash
against cliffs,

why
fog lingers
on
mountain tops,

why
wolves
howl.

even in
our unfettered freedom,
we don't
want
to be
lonely.

— there's alone and then there's loneliness

i forgot,
often,
that i wasn't
fragile.

i forgot,
often,
that you're weren't
perfect.

i'll remember
when it's all over.

— i'm happy to forget you, though

i
fall into
this
routine
of
loving myself
just enough
to survive,
but
not enough
to thrive.

i should stop.

— how does your garden grow

she
wraps herself
in darkness again,
a weighted blanket of
bliss.

everyone told her
how pretty the
light was.

no told her
how much it would hurt.

— no one tells her it's okay to love her shadow

there will be

people   places   things

that no longer
serve you,

that no longer
love you,

that no longer
know you.

learn to be okay
with leaving.

— nouns can describe hurts, too

we'll
hang the
moon,
rivers of
stardust
in our
veins,
and
pretend
space
has enough
air
for both
of us.

— young love will be the death of us

oh, baby,
she said,
you don't need me
or
a crystal ball.

gods, girl.

no.

you already
know
he's lying.

— two things that don't lie: deleted messages + fortune tellers love

—

the

raw,

held in the

dark,

open you up

kind?

it's not the
light at the
end of the
tunnel.

it's what gets
you through it.

— love is not a prize for being good

these minutes,

these hours,

these days?

they take no prisoners,

they have no reason.

we are boats

on tempest

waves.

none of us

make it out

alive.

— and we play on while the ship is sinking

we

burn leaves under the
house,

smoke out the ghosts
who've lingered too long,

change our names
so they can't come
home.

wonder why we feel alone.

— can witch doctors heal diaspora?

do you
remember
the way

your tell-tale heart

thudded
in my hand,

a harbinger
of
broken
promises?

i do.

i
should've
buried it under
floorboards, too.

— life lessons from e. a. poe

there are things
we do to
feel *alive*

and

there are things
we do to
survive,

and

sometimes
they overlap.

— and it's okay if it doesn't always make sense

some wounds don't heal right.

sometimes, we try so hard to
forget

that we
leave
a bit
of
what hurt us
still
inside
(determined to
try to grow
over
and
around it),

that we're left with scars.

— are they reminders or remainders?

untangle
the ways you
held yourself

apart,

the ways you
never felt

whole,

and

stitch yourself
anew.

— we are the makers of things

they teach us
babies
to look

both ways

before
crossing the street,

but

forget
to teach us
to keep watch
for

dangers

waiting on the
other side.

— we had to learn the hard way

i've been
thinking
about
plot twists ...

secrets.

the way
we cannot fully
know someone

until
they let us in

and

how that cracks
our hearts
wide open.

— Dimmesdale was the father, and that changed everything

i feel
like
i wait
all
year
for this,

she said,

handprint
on the
window
already
disappearing.

— we all want to be seen

talk to me about
star-crossed
lovers,

of

Cleo
and
her Roman
lover,

Romeo
and
his young
Capulet.

tell me all the ways
love keeps us alive.

tell me all the ways
love keeps us from
living.

— we all love a romantic tragedy

in surviving,
i learned
how to run,

how to save myself.

i never
learned
how to stay.

— trust is a learned behavior

she bound the rope
around her
waist,
tightly.

like arms.

like salvation.

it's easier to walk
underwater,
she knew,
when the rocks kept you
from floating away.

— sometimes it hurts to live on land

i don't wish on
stars
anymore.

they burn too brightly,

shooting across the sky
all aflame.

my dreams demand
fixed points,

and

steady hearts.

they want more.

— don't pin your dreams on stardust

it's almost winter.

is it snowing
where you are?

see,
i'm not sure
if it's just
hot here,

or

if being without
you
just *feels* like hell.

— maybe only your heart has frozen over

what's it like,

he asked,

to be vulnerable,

to bare your neck,

hold your breath
and
wait for the death blow?

a lot like love,
she said.

— we all know our executioner

we dove in
headfirst,
ignoring the

rocks
and
riptide

beneath the swells.

we did things like that,
us two.

pretending we could swim.

pretending life didn't hurt.

— we never listen to the lifeguards

at some point,
we decided
we weren't
worthy of
love.

i wonder
who
teaches us that.

i wonder
how
you break someone

so much

they'll live lies.

— witches might float, but everyone drowns

there was the way
your hand felt
at the nape of my neck,

the way it all felt
like ownership,

which felt like love

and . . .

i'm not sure i knew
the difference then.

i wish i had.

— things are so easily replaced

i can't tell you
what'll save you,
but
i can tell you
that you
are
worth saving.

— letter to my younger self and my older self and my daughter and maybe you, too

i've spent
way too many
nights
drunk off
spirits,

and

not enough
nights
communing with my
ghosts.

— we can't talk if my speech is slurred

we are

reckless hearts

playing with fire,

arsonists of lives,

and

still

we wonder where

all the scars came from.

— the pain is so familiar, we don't notice the burns

we wore
our cages
like
finery,

our white flag
hearts

bright stars
against the sea
of words
that roiled between us.

baby,
we were destined to sink.

— there's only room on that door for one of us

we are

parked cars
on deserted roads

and

hidden benches
in dark parks

and

raging rivers
after a storm.

we are
everything

we're taught
we should avoid.

— but we learn by doing

i wanted to say

he's a dumpster fire,

but i nodded along
instead,

and

wondered how long
before she realized
there are better ways
to stay warm.

– i'm sure even Cassandra bit her tongue until it bled sometimes

we'll cast shadows
by dashboard light,

and

i'll whisper my sins
into his neck . . .

pretend this is love,

watch the windows frost
with hot breath and aching.

— some confessionals have four doors

he said,

you're not like other girls.

as if that's a good thing,
as if that made her special.

and

she ate it up,
hungry for attention.

— you don't have to be a unicorn to be magical

i think
i hear you
calling my name,

honeyed syllables
dripping
off your tongue.

i am wrong.

– all my ghosts have your voice

1. the bed will be warm,
but empty.

2. i'll dance in the kitchen
by myself.

3. there'll be tears when i
follow him only to realize
he's not you.

— this is how you haunt me

my heart doesn't break

over you

anymore;

she knows better than to
trust

the words of serpents.

— and forked-tongues speak half-truths

we drove backroads,

hands reaching for
the stars

and

between thighs.

we never saw the end coming.

— we spared the trees, but not each other

he says i'm

a tsunami,

says i only leave
wreckage
in my wake.

i don't correct
him.

— i never promised him calm seas

she is
bad poetry.

like
unfinished stanzas

and

missi g lett rs.

like
finding nothing but
...
.

she made you feel
something,

you just didn't know what.

— she knows she's a work in progress

i'm in all
the in-between
spaces
these days.

the held breath.

the skipped beat.

the slip of night.

it's a wonder i am
here at all.

— sometimes we are the ghosts we hear in the walls

i think,
sometimes,
the way we

breathe

says more about
our hearts
than it does
our lungs.

— how do we exorcise our cardiovascular system

sometimes,

the moon

is just

the moon,

and

sometimes

the moon

is like that ex

you hate to love

—

the pull is strong,

sure,

but you know

you won't survive.

— there's a lesson there somewhere

*i tried so hard
to ignore the ache,*

she said,

*but shadows
aren't forgiving;*

they're just hungry.

— and we'll devour anything to not feel empty

he was a river.

you know,
the kind you
wade into,

and

realize
too late
that you're being
swept away.

— fast moving and breathtaking, he was

i locked my heart
away in a tower,

and

promised one day
to return.

i locked my heart
away in a tower

just to watch it burn.

— sometimes being the villain saves us

i take a

deep breath,

long before

the plunge,

and then

i let go

i let go

i let go.

— we're never as ready as we hope we are

curse your heart
like a tomb,

bury your secrets
like treasures.

make them
work for it,
babygirl.

— it's okay to want a tenacious explorer

there is firewater in my veins,

the kind that burns
in all the good ways

but

makes waking a mess.

my heart is
exhausted
from it all.

— who needs liquor when you can self-sabotage sober

you see,

sometimes . . .

sometimes,

when you're at the
bottom,

the life raft
looks like
just another wave.

– and simply keeping afloat is exhausting

chasing the light

doesn't drive the demons away.

no . . .

it only takes them longer to catch up.

— so, i run until my legs and lungs give out

he says

you taste like regret

when he kisses me,

but his lips are unsettled ghosts,

so it's a good thing we're both
too hungry to care.

— sugar and spice and all the things we wish we could forget she said,

*i don't think Cupid worries
about His aim.*

*maybe that's why some loves
shatter us.*

— it's all walking targets + dumb luck, isn't it

i remember the way
the syllables of my name
tumbled from his mouth,

a rush of air
like music to my ears.

who knew
music and lies
sounded the same.

— maybe all the great songwriters are just skilled liars

their lips
were petal soft.

what a wonderful way
to disguise the thorns.

— *bouquets of bad boyfriends* sounds like a band name

i looked for my heart
in empty rooms,

found only locked doors.

forgot i held the keys.

— people can be empty rooms, in case you forgot, too

i used to think we were
waves
crashing into each other.

but,
i'm convinced we were
ships.

-- all that damage, is it any surprise nothing survived?

WOLVES

— and the wild ways we choose to survive —

there are
wolves
out there,

they said.

i know,

she replied,

they
came
with
me.

— underestimated

there is

a space

in my chest,

a hollow of echoes,

where my voice resides.

she turns my whimpers

into howls.

— den

i never learned
the names
of all the
stars.

i just knew
the one
like a wolf
was

mine,

my map,

my way
back home.

to you.

— some of us are still pack animals

we'll
write stories
filtered through

what we want
rather than
what they say

and

wonder why
our ghosts
stop talking to us

and

just haunt us instead.

— there is always something lost in translation

we dance

with our demons

under the full moon,

wear mist

like

ballgowns

and

fire light

like

magic.

we are

the

revelry

we have been

waiting for.

— it's time to live deliciously

what if

our fingers

left

star

trails

instead of

bruises.

— we're far too volatile for our own good

one day,

when this

is all over,

i won't

spend a moment

regretting

that piece of cake.

— i'm done apologizing for having a body

she
excavated
the bones,

swirls of earth
leaving imprints
on her fingers,

a sign that she was there,

was willing
to get dirty

and

do the work.

— we are the tomb raiders *and* archeologists

let's sit together,
me and you,
comparing

scars

and

jagged edges.

let's marvel
at the way
we've stitched
ourselves
together.

— and all the ways we have survived

we are

the

fire

blazing,

the

earth

shaking,

the

seas

churning.

we are

the

cataclysm

and

rebirth.

– we are the moment of creation

sometimes
forgiveness
is not a balm.

sometimes
you have to
light a
match

and

watch it
burn.

— we can live in chains or rise from ashes

i used to wish
a knight
would come
save me.

until i realized
there was no
knight ...

there was just
me.

so,
i fought
and
saved
myself.

— a dress is just a pretty sheath for a sword

i tell her

he's a snake, he doesn't deserve your time,

and

then
i remember
all the tears i've cried
over boys that
slither.

and

i know
she'll have
to learn
the hard way.

we all do.

— no one could tell Eve anything either

how much of who
i am
is because of what
i've done

and

how much of who
i am
is because of what's
been done

to me.

— stop signing contracts with your blood

keep close your

oracles;

the ones who
stand in the flames
of your
catastrophes

and

don't look away.

the ones who
read your heart
back to you.

— to pray, to speak, to see

he said,

*tell me your story
in six words or less*

and

she replied,
i survived.
i survived.
i survived.

— and isn't *that* just fucking magical itself

you've been kept
small
for far
too long.

give yourself
space

to become.

to breathe.

to be.

— dig the grave a little wider, honey

if it all burns down,
what do we save?

what do we save?

what do we save?

each other.

when it's all burning,
we save each other.

— if we run, we run together

close the door

burn the bridge.

you owe them nothing.

— it's okay to walk away from what is killing you

you have
walked on your knees.

you have
watched them bleed,
watched the way
the path then became
your own.

you have
paid your penance.

stop apologizing.

— some baggage is meant to be misplaced

don't believe them
when they say

you are too much;

you'll end up
starving
while they feast.

— they keep you hungry so you'll accept scraps

strip it all away,
but
leave the scars

—

your
bare flesh
flinching
at the slightest
touch
of kindness

—

and
know,
even like this,
you are still beautiful.

— you are enough. you are enough. you are enough.

all they see is
the scorched
earth,

the barren space
once bountiful,

the way
limbs have
tangled,
turned to ash.

no one notices
the room to grow.

— don't be afraid to be a human wildfire

i'd rather
live on
the trail of crumbs,

she whispered,

than ever return
to my father's home.

— sometimes the witch in the woods *isn't* the villain

there are a
million
ways to die

(a little every day
is the worst)

and

a
million
ways to heal

(a little every day
is my favorite).

— what doesn't kill us teaches us

when i feel

lost,

i check in with my

heart

and

see it's just found

another way.

— we all carry our own true north

the truth is

none of us know
if we're doing it right,

but

we keep trying anyway

and

if that isn't magic,

i don't know what is.

— you walk me home, i'll answer your late night calls; this is how we make it

you don't have to
starve
to create good work

and

you don't have to
burn
to make magic.

you are more
than just your
story of struggle.

— safety nets are safety nets for a reason, loves

i told
the trees
about you.

i'm convinced
all this fog
is them
sighing in relief,
too.

— i've been holding my breath, i think

and
sometimes,
still,
my heart is a

coiled snake —

always searching for
warmth,

always ready to
strike.

— they call it poison, i call it protection

forgive yourself
all the times
you drowned out your
instincts,
saying yes
around teeth clenched in
no,
nodding your head
when your legs
wanted to
run,

the conditioning of

nice girl
sweet girl
pliable girl.

forgive yourself;
you know how.

— it's a learning process, i know

i wonder what sort of

warrior

it takes

to cross oceans,

to bury babies,

to fight and love
like wildfire,

so the

granddaughters
of her womb

may live better lives.

— may i never forget that i am the
   daughter of the daughter of such ferocity

when we can't
set fire
to the boat,

can't watch the pyre

burn,

we just
set fire
to the anchors.

— the ties that bind are flammable

darling,

even the

strongest,

most constant

lighthouse

still needs tending

to save others.

you are a

lighthouse.

— don't let your light wink out

i burned their
fingerprints
off my skin,

flesh apple red
—
freshly plucked
and
full of poison.

sometimes
snakes
are
boys
in baseball caps.

no one warned Eve.

— what sort of god just sits and watches *that*

one day,

i'll stop trying to find
life lessons

in the spaces
where my scars meet.

today is not that day.

— tree rings show their age; these scars show i survived

i laid there,

f i r e w o r k s

punctuating

each reach for

god.

i should've known

you could never save me.

— the grass stains hid the knife in my back

we were stairways
in lighthouses.

dark.

empty.

waiting to be used.

— and hurricane season's a lot like love

i gathered the pieces

—

a broken heart here,
a flash of trauma there

—

and remembered how

satisfying

puzzles could be.

— and i'll start with the corner(ed) parts

SIRENS

— and the many aching, enchanting, haunting things —

i tuck the bones
of who i once was
under the blanket,

a tangle of red plaid

amongst the
branches and moss,

and

remind myself
they'll be there
when i'm ready.

— less Red, more Wolf

i don't fault
Eve
for eating the
apple,

but if it were me,

i would've
harvested
the seeds
and fed
them to
Adam.

– cyanide

we are

a tangle

of limbs

and

hot

bated breath.

we are

a wildfire

just waiting

to

ignite.

— he is an arsonist

her lips are blood red

—

sweet, like you'd expect

—

but there is a bitterness
there, too.

a *bite*.

and he likes it,
likes that she is more than
what she seems.

and he likes it,
likes that her lips
taste like life,
taste like death.

— kiss me like you mean it

She knows

a story
is as good as
a prayer

is as close to
worship
as some
gods
get these days.

She knows
being remembered
is
as close to
being revered
as some
gods
get these days.

— they're starving for attention

what's it like,

they ask.

everyone wants to know
about him.

*like walking in the dark
and knowing my way.*

— Persephone's girls' weekend

i bite

it back

(the

need,

the

wanting)

until

i

taste

blood.

and then

i use it

as an

offering.

— the great [rite] now

doors
and
hearts
and
legs
and
words

open.

and,
oh,
how beautiful
the possibilities
when we step over
the threshold.

— leaps of faith in liminal spaces

the dappled light,

like morse code

on satin

skin.

a beacon.

an s.o.s.

he never

stood

a

chance.

— she is a Bermuda triangle

slip it on,
the softest leather,
and
slip away.

he knew
you were not
a woman
to tame.

he knew
the moon
would
call
you
home
someday.

— the sea is made of selkie tears

She
walks
the grey halls,

and

the earth shivers
in anticipation.

oh,
how the
days grow so
cold
when
She returns
to the
warmth of
His bed.

— who knew gods of the dead were so welcoming

but why
pigs,
they asked.

they always ask.

i don't
choose
the form,

she replied,

i just
hold
the mirror.

— when you fuck with witches

she
is
stripped
bare,

her
bloodied thighs
a sanctuary
they love
to hate.

they cry out,

who are you
to tempt us.

who are you
to stop.

– they want their virgins slutty

i keep dreaming

of corridors and
windows,
crossroads and
crooked signposts,

of dark spaces,
apple stars,
dead blooms,
the night sky.

of being
wholly
holy.

it's time.

— season of the witch

we're waiting for

the gladiators,
the heroes,
the saviors.

but

Rome is burning,

and

we're at temples
making offerings,
hoping the gods hear us,

knowing they don't.

— no one listened to Cassandra, either

i tempt Fate

and

men alike,

walking the
razor's edge
of being.

i don't
ask for their
attention,

don't invite it,

but
they sharpen
their scissors
anyway.

– they control all the strings

because,

sometimes
their broken hearts
are better than
your surrender.

— if Helen of Troy gave out advice

you are

more

than just

ruins.

so,

remember

the ways they

worshipped

you

and

bring your

temple

back to

life.

— you are the faith you've lost

she is

the siren

and

the shipwreck.

she is
why he

wants.

she is
why he

drowns.

– come, let me sing you a song of destruction

one day,
i stopped being
the heroine
of everyone else's
story

and

realized
i'd rather be
the villain.

no one expects her to
smile
when she's hurting.

– i owe you nothing

he thought
he heard
her say,

i
don't like the
drowning...

but
i do love the
quiet.

— everything has its price

the veil

thins

and

the words

just

won't

stop,

so
i meet them
at the crossroads
like we're
old friends.

— my muse walks with ghosts

i'm sorry for the way
my words
turned into

poison-tipped barbs,

for the way
they clung to you

like claws.

sometimes . . .

sometimes,
i don't know my own strength.

sometimes . . .

sometimes
i don't recognize my own pain.

— i don't know how *not* to hurt first, but i'm trying

i used to dream of poison on my lips,

of altars to my heart
burning
like bonfires left

untended.

but

poison isn't as sweet
as they
want you
to think,

and

the fires
never burn
hot enough.

— these violent delights have violent ends

under the twinkling lights,
she seemed

less hellion

and

more heaven.

he wasn't sure
which
he preferred.

— she knew, so she turned off the lights

*stars don't make for
proper bedfellows,*

she whispered
against the expanse
of his back,

*but you
seek me out
anyway.*

— we'll burn up like the sun, but you'll ask for more

honey,
don't ever let someone tell you
what you are —

who you are.

you breathe fire.

you crack thunder.

you are the ocean
in a human vessel.

— you are too much to be contained by someone else's
opinions; be too much

we talk about
bodies
as if they are

things

and not

sentient beings

waiting
to be invited
into the conversation.

— seen and not heard

they said,

*her teeth will
draw blood.*

they said,

*some nights you'll
barely catch the sound
of her escape.*

they said,

*she only speaks
a language of sin.*

they said,

*when you bed
a monster,
you become
a good actor*

or

a co-conspirator.

choose wisely, child.

— we all want to play house with witches until they actually move in

and
she sheds

lives

like
snake skins.

— don't stop outgrowing yourself

his hands
spread my thighs
like
the holy grail
opens lips,

and

he murmurs my name,
appealing to the gods.

— and all the holy ways we save ourselves

tell me about the way she
sank her teeth
into ripe flesh,
the way juice
dripped from her lips

and

all he could do
was stand there

aghast

. . .

and
aching.

— they'll tell you he didn't want to leave eden with her; they lie

they say she was

wild,
unruly,
unrepentant.

they say that she

breathed fire,
and
drew blood.

they say a lot of things.

this time, they aren't lying.

— she is unapologetically made of wolf claws and dragon scales

i was taught

to present

perfect posture

far more than

i was taught

to honor

the power of my

no.

— and they wonder why we don't speak up

i brought myself to
the shoreline,

reminded myself

here. this is where it happens.

i knew
it would be heavy
—
the wait
of being
home
—

and

i dove in
anyway.

— the tides aren't the only ones that need to shift

he tastes

like
blood magic

and

fairy circles,

like mead
on my lips.

he is why
i wait at
crossroads.

— there are no words for that kind of love

i feel her
pacing,
in the space
between

breath and beat,

and

thank the gods
for ribcages.

— sometimes my heart is a wayward wolf

because
every island
swallowed
whole
reminds me why
i'd rather be the

waves

than be the

waiting.

— ask mermaids; they know

it was the way
she made promises
she never meant to keep,

swore
this was how to love —
just enough to
keep the wolves from the door.

— no, baby, no; you have to invite them in

i've no need for
the marble
temple.

i am the
ruins,

the caved oracle.

i am what i came for.

— you don't need to look like them to be sacred

baby,

it is not enough to learn

to swim

against the currents

if you forget

to breathe.

— mermaids and sailors await saviors alike

each month,
red runs
from the house
once held by her
grandmother,

the moans
and
growls

so close,

she knows
they must be
inside her.

red runs,

and

she knows
huntsmen

are afraid of
her,

afraid of
the girl
who turns into
a wolf
but doesn't die.

— so, they use an axe to "save" her

pluck a snake
from your hair,

darling,

and

tie it around
your knees.

tell the gods
you love being

frightening.

tell them
pretty
got you

nothing

but

pain.

tell them you know
even

water

can be poison.

— Medusa knew the curse of patriarchy well

don't let them forget
who you really are,

queen.

with your name
on their lips

long before

he laid waste
to your heart,

you are

more than a

trophy.

you are

more than

jealousy.

you are

more than

an afterthought.

— Hera is painted on walls older than words

blessed are the
orgy of limbs,
hands
reaching,

starlit
skies
against a backdrop of
fire.

blessed are the
children of the
moon,
clothed in nothing but
earth,

doused
in magic.

— may your Beltane fires ever burn bright, lovelies

leave a cup of
water on your night stand,

and

bells on your door.

they'll come calling,
my dear.

you'll want to hear
and
they'll be thirsty.

— necromancy 101

her body
is a
book of the
dead,

the ghosts of
her lived lives
haunting her
heart,

her lips
a cursed tomb
waiting for the right
explorer.

— you see, pretty words won't be enough

be brutal,
darling.

be a knife fight.
be a rogue wave.

don't be afraid to snarl,
dear.

— in the making of little girls, don't forget the mettle

i laid my head against
His chest

(an echo chamber of
lust and loss,

the place those seeds took root),

and wondered what
Mother would think
of my new favorite lullaby.

— Demeter's daughter is a master gardener

speak the words

and

shed your skin.

leave your gifts
at the gate.

watch what blooms

from the bleeding.

learn where your

scars

make you stronger.

— rebirth: a how-to

i don't know what else to say.

maybe i'm all out of demons.

— what happens in the aftermath of healing?

LIGHTHOUSES

— and all the loves that save us —

and
i'm not sure
if that's

your heart beating

or

mine,

but

we're alive,

and

that's all that
really matters.

— we fought so hard to be here

sometimes i'm
not sure if
my heart is
a wolf
or
a moon;

all i know
is all of me
wants to curve
around you
in the dark.

— maybe it's a little of both

i think

whoever decided

sleep deprivation

was

 torture

must have been

sleeping

without you,

too.

– Geneva convention

in
a
room
full
of
books,
it's
his
spine
that
begs
to
be
beneath
her
fingers.

— braille

if you are

the dark depths,

all rough seas

and rumble

of waves

echoing

to

the stars,

i want

to be

the

lighthouse,

i want

to be

home

home

home.

— seaworthy

your words are not

k n i v e s,

your hands are not

c h a i n s,

your bones are not

a c a g e.

i don't
flinch
when you
love
me.

– this is what saves me

we fold ourselves
into each other,

fingers fumbling,

roaming,

and

i learn
why hands press
together
in prayer.

— holy communion

we lie there,

legs draped like velvet
on bare skin.

i tell him
i want to hold the stars
in my hand,

fireflies pulsing against
the night sky,

and

he sighs,

tells me the fireflies
miss me, too.

— field of dreams

our

hands roaming

in the dark

like long shadows

reaching across

heated pavement,

like the tide

swallowing,

whole,

the shore.

— we're all hungry for more

and the night tastes

like

sweet nothings
whispered on
clavicles
slick with sweat,

like

crisp sheets
waiting to be
rumpled,

like

an inferno raging
under my
skin.

— your mouth is a three course meal

let's stay up late,

mouths hot with want

hands mapping the stars
—
supernovas between our thighs.

i'm too awake to sleep.

i'm so tired of saying no.

— we are heavenly bodies in motion

sometimes,

we drift

with

each other,

two currents

with

the same

destination.

sometimes,

we crash

into

each other,

two storms

with

nowhere else

to go.

and, still.

— i'd rather drown with you than without you

what's your green light,

he whispered
against
my neck.

i'm . . .
i'm not sure,

i said out loud,

while my heart
pleaded
with every beat

you

you

you.

— i get why Gatsby bootlegged

he tells me
momma,
it's a journal
about my life,

and

i think
about how
beautiful
it is
that he already
knows
his stories
are worth
remembering.

— my six-year-old, the writer

oh, how
i want
to
keep you,

baby
mine,

but

wolves
weren't meant
for
cages,

boats
weren't made
for
harbors.

— the door is open, the light is on

and the words?

oh, they become

a bone
singing

a breath
giving

a blood-
letting.

and,

i concede,

this is far better
than the alternative
ways of relief.

— they save me from myself

there is

a stirring

in my

blood

—

a spinning

top,

a whirling

dervish

—

each time

your lips

press

against mine.

— we defy the laws of physics

he lays hands on me,

a healing pilgrimage
in his fingertips.

he is the

words of my throat.
smoke in my lungs.
oil on my lips.

he is

the body.

the blood.

and

i am the altar.

– and, oh, how beautiful he is on his knees

our

bare skin

and

bared teeth,

and

all the ways we love
like

wild

leaves me breathless.

— open my mouth, fill my lungs

i am a map of
restlessness,

an aching expanse
of explorable emptiness.

and your rose-heart
is my only compass.

— you are all the ways i find home

there are no
no words
for the way

we love.

there is just
the way

we conjure

magic,

you and i.

bodies warm,

our breaths

rumbling
thunder
in the dark,

our hands
like

lightning

waiting to strike.

– you are my favorite kind of storm

you'll be the sun,

scorched edges
but fixed point,

and

i'll be the midnight quilt,

my chest all the north stars,

my thighs a collection of
supernovas.

— each constellation a space of aching

there's this way
your breath

catches,

strangled words
rushing from
your lips,

that convinces me
there must be a
heaven.

— you make my name sound like a prayer

i love you
on your knees,

lips moving
in fervent prayer
against altars of flesh,

and

the way
my name
sounds
like a hymn
in between breaths.

— there are so many ways to worship

he met me
somewhere
between

the fire

and

the forests,

waited with his hand outstretched,
palm open.

knew he didn't have to tame me
to love me.

— trust

no one told us
that,

sometimes,

it'd feel
like we're speaking
different languages;

that we'd become

foreign

to each other

if we weren't dedicated to
meeting halfway.

– our bedroom walls are passport pages

they thought the earth was
flat,

and

i thought i'd always be
broken.

we were both wrong.

— it's okay to fall off the edge; it's not the end of the world

he anoints her with oils,

sings praises to her hips,

and

kisses her feet at the altar.

— this is how he knows god

there are
far too many
nights
when the

wolf
in me

longs for the
sight
of you.

— i am convinced you are the moon

she said,

i don't always love

myself

so, sometimes,
i need you to
love me
for the both of us.

— life lesson: use your words and ask for what you need

i place my hands
on his chest
like warming them
in front of a
fire,

trusting he won't burn me.

— he promises my skin doesn't smell like smoke anymore

our monsters

love each other

so well

we can't remember

why we were ever afraid

of falling.

— this is what happens when we stop running from nothing

good love

can help

reframe

our stories.

— and it doesn't have to come from ourselves first

bodies slick
like rain soaked roads

and

i know . . .

i know you'll be the death of me.

— you make me reckless

he looks at me
like

i'm a glass of water

and

he's been lost
in the desert,

and

i kiss his neck

and

swear to him
he smells like rain.

— when he walked in

take a lover

who thinks you are

more than

magic.

take a lover

who knows the

battlefield

is your mind,

but

meets you in the

trenches

anyway.

— the difference between exes and allies

when everything is relative,

even the shortest distance

(your lips almost on mine)

feels too far away.

— point A to point B, right

love

should allow you to

sink

into someone without

suffocating.

— it's not enough to be left breathless

i remind myself

we are all made of star dust,

hoping your stars someday align with mine.

— you'll make the darkness seem less lonely

we'll recite our vows,

maybe even
slice our palms
and
make a blood oath,

weaving our pinkies together.

basically, make promises
time will never let us keep.

– one of us will be left behind; i hope it's not me

ACKNOWLEDGEMENTS

To my social media friends. Your encouragement and engagement means the world to me. Thank you for wanting these words in your hands.

To my advance readers: Cassie, Cat, Marybeth, and Melissa. Thank you for your eyes, your love, and your time. Thank you for seeing me.

To Sara. Without your endless support, enthusiastic cheerleading, patient handholding, and unwavering belief, these words would not be in a book. I could not have done this without you, friend.

And finally, but most importantly, to Eric, Jazell, Ethan, and Owen. The love of my life. Mes petits loups. The ones who found me, the ones who saved me, the ones who keep me from getting swept away. Thank you for being my lighthouse in the storm, my north star even on the darkest of nights, my endless supply of poetry. Thank you for loving me so well.

AUTHOR

Wife. Mama wolf.

Heathen. Moon lover. Oracle. Tattoo collector. Witch.

Nicole Colinarez most often writes under the pseudonym Nicole Sea.

Blog: thewildinbetween.com
Email inquiries: thewildinbetween@gmail.com
Instagram: @thewildinbetween

The Wild In-Between, 1st ed. Copyright © 2018 by Nicole Colinarez. All rights reserved. No part of this book may be altered, distributed, reproduced, transmitted, or used in any manner whatsoever without written permission except in the case of brief quotations embodied in critical reviews and certain other noncommercial uses permitted by copyright law.

— — —

Paper Lion Press

www.paperlionpress.com

Cover art by Nicole Colinarez. Title font is Bellamy. Content font is Bodoni 72.

www.ingramcontent.com/pod-product-compliance
Lightning Source LLC
Chambersburg PA
CBHW031939110426
42744CB00029B/207